Financial Sanity

In Three Easy Lessons

The Fiscal Fitness Company, Inc.
www.tffco.com
ISBN: 978-0-9899016-1-1

This book is dedicated to God and my family, both of whom keep me focused on the right things in life. May I always listen to them and heed their counsel. And may they forgive me for all the times that I fail to do so.

Financial Sanity
In Three Easy Lessons

BY

DAVID G. SIMPSON, J.D.

REGISTERED INVESTMENT ADVISOR

2013

TABLE OF CONTENTS

"Blessed is the rich man that is found without blemish: and that hath not gone after gold, nor put his trust in money nor in treasures. Who is he, and we will praise him? For he hath been tried thereby, and made perfect, he shall have glory everlasting. He that could have transgressed, and hath not transgressed: and could do evil things, and hath not done them: Therefore are his goods established in the Lord, and all the church of the saints declare his alms."

From the deuterocanonical book, Ecclesiasticus (Sirach) 31:8-11.

LESSON ONE: THE PROPER PERSPECTIVE

Some years ago I attended the funeral of the wife of a good friend. As I waited to offer my condolences, I watched a slide-show of their life together and was impressed at how handsome my friend had been in his youth and how much his younger self had resembled the icon of his age: Elvis Presley.

When my turn came to speak to him, after offering my regrets for his loss, I tried to lighten the mood with the remark that I loved the pictures of his earlier life and thought that he had missed his calling and should have been a rock and roll star. Without missing a beat my friend replied, "No, I should've been a preacher."

I knew what he meant. In some sense, we all should spend our lives working for eternal truths rather than what occupies too much of our time and talents. Worse still is how easily we make the things we do in work (or the money we make at it) into a god in place of the One we supplanted. Please indulge me as I preach.

Every finance book I have ever read suffers from one of two FATAL flaws. The first flaw, the theological flaw, can be rather simply expressed as one which makes money into God. The second flaw, the philosophical flaw, makes money the source of one's happiness.

Both are demonstrably false, especially when stated in such plain language. But because we live in such a materialistic culture, it is surprising how often those two flaws continue to insinuate themselves into the thinking of the common man.

Lesson One is meant as a corrective to those errors. However, like all fundamental inquiries, Lesson One is not a lesson that one learns once and masters, but rather one that must be continually re-visited, plumbed for greater depth and willed into one's financial life.

The good news is that you already know Lesson One. Like all fundamental truths, it is simple, profound and readily intelligible. Lesson One is all about keeping the proper perspective about money and can be easily stated like this: Money is not God and is not the source of happiness. In short, Lesson One is the refutation of the two fatal flaws mentioned above. All POSITIVE financial planning must begin with one's simple affirmation of Lesson One.

Later in this book, I will begin detailing many technical aspects about finance and how better to manage money. But if you should ever start to wonder about the purpose of all the specifics that I set forth, re-read this chapter. Lesson One is the alpha and the omega of all human action. Lessons Two and Three are forever contingent upon Lesson One. Lose sight of Lesson One and the rest of your efforts will come to naught.

Ask 100 people if they have made money their God and you will get a near unanimous, "NO!" Their adamancy comes from their sincerity.

But probe a bit deeper and a strange pre-occupation comes into focus. One man wants to accumulate a substantial fortune so "his kids won't have to work like he did." Another person wants to accumulate a handsome sum to be secure and free from the exigencies of life. Still another says, "If I had a million bucks, I would...."

No work, security and all the things money can buy! These have become the quest of the modern man...through money. And they are as unachievable through money as they are fallacious in their reasoning.

In the ages of faith, it was known and accepted that a person could not escape the Divine judgment that human beings would "labour and toil...all the days of [their] life."[1] Further, even if someone had enough money to believe that they no longer had to labor to produce, their toil becomes their worry about keeping that nest-egg so their "non-working" condition persists. In my experience, these people are pretty miserable with worry.

Money equals security? How many stories do we need to hear of the "lottery winner gone broke" or the "millionaire athlete

---

[1] Genesis 3:17

passing away" before we reject this lie? Again the people of the ages of faith would have offered a simple, but true, corrective: "Our help is in the name of the Lord, who made heaven and earth."[2]

Oddly, it is the third delusion, namely that money will enable us to buy all the things we want and need to be happy, which is the most enduring despite a long-standing axiom that says the exact opposite: "Money can't buy happiness." But we don't need the ancient philosophers[3] or Ebenezer Scrooge to confirm this for us. All we need do is look at the things we have accumulated in life and ask, "Which of these has made me (and continues to make me) happy?" Or more to the point, if you were going to spend the rest of your life on a deserted island, would you want some THING or someONE to spend it with?

Lay not up to yourselves treasures on earth: where the rust, and moth consume, and where thieves break through and steal. But lay up to yourselves treasures in heaven: where neither the rust nor moth doth consume, and where thieves do not break through, nor steal. For where thy treasure is, there is thy heart also....No man can serve two masters. For either he will hate the one, and love the other: or he will sustain the one, and despise the other. You cannot serve God and mammon. Therefore I say to you, be not solicitous for your life, what you shall eat, nor for your body, what you shall put on. Is not the life more than the meat: and the body more than the raiment? Behold the birds of the air, for they neither sow, nor do they reap, nor gather into barns: and your heavenly Father

---

[2] Psalms 123:8; See also Psalms 145:5, "Blessed is he who hath the God of Jacob for his helper, whose hope is in the Lord his God."
[3] See for example Socrates' explanation in Georgias p. 34.

feedeth them. Are not you of much more value than they? And which of you by taking thought, can add to his stature by one cubit? And for raiment why are you solicitous? Consider the lilies of the field, how they grow: they labour not, neither do they spin. But I say to you that not even Solomon in all his glory was arrayed as one of these. And if the grass of the field, which is today, and tomorrow is cast into the oven, God doth so clothe: how much more you, O ye of little faith? Be not solicitous therefore, saying, What shall we eat: or what shall we drink, or wherewith shall we be clothed? For after all these things do the heathens seek. For your Father knoweth that you have need of all these things. Seek ye therefore first the kingdom of God, and his justice, and all these things shall be added unto you. Be not therefore solicitous for tomorrow; for the morrow will be solicitous for itself. Sufficient for the day is the evil thereof.[4]

---

[4] Matthew 6:19 and following.

Still, the solution to the materialism of our age is not necessarily the eschewing of all property, but rather keeping the proper perspective on material things. In short, the solution to materialism is not anti-materialism, but spirituality.

Here are some concrete suggestions on how to keep the proper perspective on money and material blessings:

- Tithe. Giving away a portion of your earnings to support your Church, its pastors and their mission is the surest way to keep a detached attitude towards the goods of this world.

- Tithe of yourself. We used to call these the spiritual and corporal works of mercy, but it is really nothing more than giving of yourself in charity. Visit the sick in the hospital, help your elderly neighbor, volunteer at a food bank or counsel the incarcerated. The list is endless and blessedness is sure to come to those who give love.

- Practice liberality. This virtue calls us to be free in our spending, especially in the hiring of others. The idea here is to detach from our wealth, not to hold it in such high regard that we never want to spend it. We are not spending for spending sake, but are freeing our spirit to spend willingly and joyfully on all the essentials of life and the services of our neighbors.

- Fast regularly. Denying oneself the goods of this world is the surest way to begin to appreciate the value of the next.

Further, denying oneself the legitimate pleasures of life will strengthen us and make us less susceptible to the temptations of the illegitimate pleasures of life, also known as sin.

- Pray and meditate regularly. The growth of the spiritual component in our lives will necessarily produce a lessening of the hold materiality has on us.

A man going into a far country, called his servants, and delivered to them his goods; And to one he gave five talents, and to another two, and to another one, to every one according to his proper ability: and immediately he took his journey

And he that had received the five talents, went his way, and traded with the same, and gained other five. And in like manner he that had received the two, gained other two. But he that had received the one, going his way digged into the earth, and hid his lord's money. But after a long time the lord of those servants came, and reckoned with them. And he that had received the five talents coming, brought other five talents, saying: Lord, thou didst deliver to me five talents, behold I have gained other five over and above.

His lord said to him: Well done, good and faithful servant, because thou hast been faithful over a few things, I will place thee over many things: enter thou into the joy of thy lord. And he also that had received the two talents came and said: Lord, thou deliverest two talents to me: behold I have gained other two. His lord said to him: Well done, good and faithful servant: because thou hast been faithful over a few things, I will place thee over many things: enter thou into the joy of thy lord. But he that had received the one talent, came and said: Lord, I know that thou art a hard man; thou reapest where thou hast not sown, and gatherest where thou hast not strewed. And being afraid I went and hid thy talent in the earth: behold here thou hast that which is thine. And his lord answering, said to him: Wicked and slothful servant, thou knewest

19

that I reap where I sow not, and gather where I have not strewed: Thou oughtest therefore to have committed my money to the bankers, and at my coming I should have received my own with usury. Take ye away therefore the talent from him, and give it to him that hath ten talents. For to every one that hath shall be given, and he shall abound: but from him that hath not, that also which he seemeth to have shall be taken away. And the unprofitable servant cast ye out into the exterior darkness. There shall be weeping and gnashing of teeth. **Matthew 25:14-30**

It might be argued that the last thing we need is another self-help book. I couldn't agree more! Moreover, in the area of financial services, the industry is so over-run with radio show pundits and easy-money infomercials that it's a wonder anyone is even listening anymore.

The "expert" advice being bandied about through the internet, radio and print media ranges from the technical, to the arcane, to pie-in-the-sky, to the legitimate. Some of it is good. Much of it is bad, contradictory or just plain wrong. In short, there is so much advice and such a confusion of ideas that people have grown tired of it.

But the counter-revolution to the "information age" has already begun. More and more people are eschewing the financial "gurus" and their sure-fire "systems" and are instead searching for basic, common-sense answers. Plus, they are ready to work to achieve their goals, but don't know where to begin.

That is what I hope to provide in this book. It really is nothing more than an accumulation of the traditional, tried and true means of being financially sound. It is common sense ordered to be more readily learned and implemented. This is so much the case that, after seeing my whole program, one client complained to me, "You are just making me save!" To which I replied (somewhat dumbstruck and taken aback): "Yes! And that's bad because?"

But, as we all know, it's not so easy to save! If it were, I wouldn't be writing this book and you wouldn't be reading it. So let's set forth an integrated financial plan. I don't intend to offer details on the mechanics of each step, but will supply, where available, further sound resources for your use.

There are four areas of a sound financial plan and each has three sub-sets. These are:

A. Money Management - Budgeting, Savings Program and Debt Management
B. Emergency Preparation - Provisions, Savings and Proper Insurance
C. Financial Stability - Intrinsic Worth Items, Alternate Earnings Method and Passive Income Generators
D. Future Planning - Retirement Funding, Education Funding and Tax Reduction

I assess a client's achievement of these issues by a "Financial Report Card" that I've created.

Financial Report Card

	2013	2014	2015	2016	2017	2018	2019	2020	2021	2022
Money Management										
Budget										
Savings Program (IBC)										
Debt Management										
Section Score	0	0	0	0	0	0	0	0	0	0
Emergency Preparation										
Emergency Provisions										
Emergency Savings										
Proper Insurance										
Section Score	0	0	0	0	0	0	0	0	0	0
Financial Stability										
Intrinsic Worth Items										
Alt. Earning Method										
PIGs (Diversify Earnings)										
Section Score	0	0	0	0	0	0	0	0	0	0
Future Planning										
Retirement Funding										
Education Funding										
Tax Reduction										
Section Score	0	0	0	0	0	0	0	0	0	0
Total Score	0.00	0.00	0.00	0.00	0.00	0.00	0.00	0.00	0.00	0.00
Grade	0.00	0.00	0.00	0.00	0.00	0.00	0.00	0.00	0.00	0.00
Bonus: Making A Difference										
Cost of Freedom										
MRI										
Charitable Giving										
Section Score	0	0	0	0	0	0	0	0	0	0

Net Worth Snapshot

Total Assets	Total Liabilities	Approximate Net Worth	% Gain Over Last Yr.
$0	$0	$0	#DIV/0!

Net Worth By Year:							

Financial Report Card

We'll discuss each of these in more detail in a moment, but first let me make an observation about modern financial planning as it relates to these four categories.

Building wealth requires multiple skills that are acquired over time and which have a sequenced order. To use an analogy, gymnasts learn how to do somersaults and handstands before they are able to do handsprings. Further, it is not until the gymnasts have mastered these simple primary moves that they are able to do Olympic runs on the floor exercise. This is just common sense!

Good financial planning is no different. A person should make sure that they are practicing good "money management" skills before they address "emergency preparation" or "future planning". However, most modern financial planning ignores this reality and focuses nearly all of its attention on "future planning" (at least the part known as "retirement planning").

Yes, there are those planners who hit on parts of "emergency planning" and some who give short shrift to "money management," but the overwhelming tendency of financial service representatives and firms is to "go where the money is" and leave the client to fend for himself on most of these foundational issues.

This is a bad idea and nearly always leads to problems…Imagine a gymnast doing a floor exercise without ever having learned how to flip! Or run?!?

So let's look at each area and the skills that underlie them.

If we asked 10 people what is the first rule of money management, most, if not all, would say a good budget. And they would be correct!

But if we asked those same 10 people if they had a good, functioning budget, probably 3 or less would say yes. That is the strange dilemma I encounter routinely in my financial planning practice.

Let's face it, budgets have a bad rap. They are not fun, not sexy and rather boring. In this fast-paced, instant gratification society, budgets are, well...the opposite! "Budgets are passé," goes the refrain, but nothing could be further from the truth. In fact, it is precisely IN a fast-paced, instant gratification environment when a budget is most needed.

But budgeting is difficult. It requires teamwork. If everyone is not in on holding to the budget, it will fail. Budgets require communication. Reminders to each other about the value and goals of the budget are critical. Budgets require flexibility. You cannot let the first set-back get you discouraged and then quit. Budgets require love, sacrifice and commitment. One advisor said, "Another problem [with budgeting] is becoming legalistic and inflexible. Then the budget becomes a family weapon instead of a family tool."[5]

---

[5] Larry Burkett, *The Financial Planning Workbook, A Family Budgeting Guide* (Christian Financial Concepts 1990), p. 9.

However, "nothing good comes easy," so the saying goes, and the values of budgeting are so enormous as to considerably outweigh any obstacles one might encounter in implementing one.

The first value is simple and plain: A budget enables you to spend less than you make. This is so fundamental and essential. How will you ever save any money UNLESS you spend less than you make? A second value of budgeting is control. Most clients feel a great deal of satisfaction in telling their money where to go RATHER than having the bills tell them where it went! Finally, peace of mind is another major value of budgeting. Establishing a system that ensures that your needs are well provided while saving for future wants and desires is very reassuring. Plus, a good budget builds in plans for emergency spending, further enhancing your peace of mind.

The best means I have found to both avoid the pitfalls of bad budgeting and acquire all the values of good budgeting is to use the age-old "envelope" system. This method is well described in the resources I have cited.

Start your budget today because it will be the foundation of all future financial success!

Budgeting Resources:

1. *The Financial Planning Workbook, A Family Budgeting Guide*, Larry Burkett.

2. *The Catholic Answers Guide to Family Finances*,
   Phil Lenahan.

3. Crown Financial Ministries, (www.crown.com)
   website/budgeting calculators.

If you have been successful with your budget, then you could enter that elite group of Americans who can save at a level that actually increases wealth.[6] Truly, saving is the key to growing wealthy.

But once you have money to tuck away, the really difficult financial questions arise. The two most obvious ones are:

1.   Where should you store the money? and
2.   How/when should you use the money?

When I practiced in the mainstream financial services industry, I noticed that they answered both questions with one response: Retirement Accounts. Store the money in an Individual Retirement Account and use the money at retirement.

And they offered some good reasons for doing this, such as:

- You are prudently saving for future security;
- You get tax deductions and tax deferral;

---

[6] http://www.deseretnews.com/article/865554710/A-quarter-of-Americans-wont-save-money-this-year.html?pg=all;
http://www.huffingtonpost.com/2012/03/30/personal-saving-rate_n_1391333.html;
http://www.cbsnews.com/8301-500395_162-57459596/survey-half-of-americans-have-insufficient-emergency-savings-quarter-have-none-at-all/;
http://www.gobankingrates.com/savings-account/64-percent-americans-1000-emergency-savings/

- You benefit from compounding interest and capital appreciation;
- Your savings are on "auto-pilot"; and
- You are discouraged from tapping into the money due to penalties and interest.

Fine reasons to be sure; however, as I dealt with real clients and their regular, ongoing financial issues, I found that they usually had need of those savings LONG before retirement rolled around. Further, storing money in their retirement accounts prompted them into becoming permanent debtors. Let's face it; if most of your assets are locked up in penalty and tax-laden investments, then your only source of funds for big-ticket items is the loan officer at a bank.

The fancy name for this problem is "liquidity risk," that is the locking up of money in an investment that you can't tap into. But as I considered the issue more closely, I realized that EVERY client is going to need **some** cash, on **some** day, for **some** reason without **some** penalties and taxes. It was foolhardy to decide that some money could be set away for "retirement" since that same money usually represented all of their savings. Every person needs liquidity. So where should we store these liquid assets?

And my clients had other monetary needs and desires. They wanted a decent return on their investments. They usually didn't like to lose money or be too risky with it. They liked the idea of tax deductibility and deferral, if they could get it. Some wanted asset protection so their life savings couldn't vanish in one lawsuit. But mostly they wanted to maintain control of their wealth without rules, taxes and penalties for using it.

That question, "What is the best place to store money?" kept coming back to me. So I went looking for an answer. I looked at banking products, brokerage/market assets, legal arrangements (trusts, family limited partnerships etc.) and even "off shore" arrangements. These all failed for various reasons. They might suffer from low returns, poor tax treatment or no asset protection. Or they failed due to inconsistent returns, too much risk or lack of control. In short, every investment or planning arrangement that I uncovered suffered from one or more fatal flaws that my clients and I were simply not willing to settle for.

Fortunately, it was around this time that I was introduced to a financial planning strategy that addressed all of these concerns AND suggested a remarkable place to store money. The strategy was called "becoming your own banker" and the storage vehicle was whole life insurance! (Don't laugh. I didn't believe it at first either until I ran one comparison after another against this product and finally had to wave the white flag and accept that I had missed the "best place to store money" simply because I did not know how to use it.)

Again, I am not going to detail the mechanics of how the "be your own banker" system works. I will leave that to your discovery through the resources I provide. But let's take a moment to review those two critical questions that arise after you are able to save money:

1. Where should you store money?

Answer: A particular type of whole life insurance.[7]

2. How/when should you use the money?

Answer: Whenever you need the money, so long as you follow the strategy and principles of "being your own banker."

As Nelson Nash, the founder of the "be your own banker" system, once told me: "Everyone should be in two businesses: The one where they earn their living and the banking business."

Savings Program Resources:

1. http://infinitebanking.org/store/#ecwid:category=136
    7505&mode=product&product=5840086
2. http://infinitebanking.org/
3. http://financialsanityin3lessons.blogspot.com/

---

[7] Some skeptics will maintain that "whole life" is the worst place to store money. I welcome the dispute. But if any reader has reservations about storing money in a life insurance contract, I will simply say this: Forget the product and store money wherever you see fit, but USE the strategy of "becoming your own banker." That is the critical component, the product is secondary. That said, the life insurance will give you the best bang for your buck.

This might come as a shocker to some, but your goal in good financial planning is not to get out of debt. The reason that is not the goal is because it is an impossibility[8].

In point of fact, we live under a fiscal and monetary regime that is DEBT based. Whether or not you understand the implications of that statement, you must come to understand this: Under the current economic system, you are NEVER out of debt. For practical, theoretical and actual reasons, this is so.

Practically, your next debt is your NEXT emergency or NEXT major purchase. In other words, if you are "debt-free" now, you won't be the moment you encounter an unexpected or large expense. Even IF your emergency fund handles the first misstep, you then have a DEBT to replenish your emergency fund or else you won't be able to handle the next one.

In the theoretical realm, advisors will tell you that if you spend CASH to avoid debt then you have just created a reverse debt. They call it "lost opportunity" and the idea is that the cash you spent (an appreciating asset) to buy an item and avoid debt (usually on depreciating assets) has just lost the opportunity to grow for the rest of your life. Maybe that's why the car dealers are

---

[8] This statement and this entire section is predicated upon the fact that we live in debt-based, inflationary monetary system. See G. Edward Griffin's book for details on this. However, if we lived under a sound currency system, then I would follow my colleagues in their advice and advise my clients to "get out of debt." As it stands now, though, that advice just sets people up for failure.

willing to "give" you ZERO percent interest?!? Once they have your capital, they have what matters, the asset, and you have a hunk of junk in a few years!

But the real and most destructive reason that you are never out of debt is this: If you are saving money, you are losing...unless you do it right. You see, when you save money at one percent interest and then experience four percent inflation, you have just gone in reverse by three percent...and that is just using the stated percent of inflation. Many experts think that real inflation is MUCH higher.

So the reason you should not try to "get out of debt" is because that course will not get you where you want or believe you are going!

Sadly, there is no REAL solution under our current monetary system. But you can take on a strategy and technique that will help you harness the power of the debt economy and use it (somewhat) to your own advantage. This is what the "becoming your own banker" system, which we discussed in the last section, is all about. And it goes a long way to making you financially sane because you stop chasing the financial chimera of "debt freedom" and instead focus on the much more fruitful course of debt management.

Simply put, debt management is the two-step process of:

1. Building up a capital reserve (this ties in and is accomplished by the earlier "savings program" concept); and then

2. Financing your own big-ticket items i.e. using your own money for big purchases and never again using an outside creditor for your revolving credit needs.

Debt Management Resources:

1. *The Creature from Jekyll Island,* G. Edward Griffin, for an explanation of our monetary policy and its impact on our financial system.

We now move to the second major component of a sound financial plan: Emergency Preparations. This section has three components as well, Provisions, Savings and Insurance, which we will detail in order.

When I was a little boy, I got mad at my parents and decided to run away from home. So I got my suitcase, threw in a change of clothes and a peanut butter and jelly sandwich, and headed down the road. (I believe my mother helped me by making the sandwich though she seemed a bit too eager for me to leave!)

Well after I had gone a block or so, getting increasingly puzzled and dumbstruck that no one in my family had chased me down to beg me to return, I decided to take a break, sit on the side of the road and eat my sandwich. I guess I thought this might give my family more time to realize the BIG mistake they were making letting me leave!

As I sat their munching on my sandwich, a stark realization hit me: This is the last meal I've got and I don't have a way to get another! So after finishing my sandwich, I slinked back home with the realization that maybe having parents wasn't so bad after all.

Now if a 5-year old boy can realize that it is wise to have some emergency provisions just in case he has no other means of support, why is it that the full-grown adults in modern America

35

scoff at such a proposal? Why too don't more financial advisors insist that their clients develop this reserve?

This concept really came to the fore when Hurricane Katrina decimated the gulf coast. In my hometown (just north of New Orleans), every road was impassable, every business was closed, the electricity was out and communications were nearly impossible. My home was without power for over 3 weeks and the overall destruction took months to ameliorate.

So could you provide for your family for 3 weeks to a month without outside assistance? I have a confession to make: I couldn't. We were able to drive to Baton Rouge to buy fuel, food and other essentials. But what if that were not possible? What if the dire conditions were more widespread?

When I draw this picture for prospective clients and ask them what they would do in such a circumstance, they usually lean forward in their chairs and ask in hushed tones, "What do you think is going to happen?" To which I reply, "I don't know! That is why we ought to plan for it."

There is a false sense of security in America. Yes, we have been richly blessed with prosperity and relative peace, but is this guaranteed forever? To me, it is just a matter of common sense that we ought to be prepared for any and every eventuality. But when the truth hit me that I had NOT done enough to prepare to take care of my wife and children when a natural disaster struck, I vowed to remedy that. It is an ongoing process.

To accomplish this in your financial plan, think "survivalist." There are plenty of websites to help you along. Here are a few that I've found worthwhile:

- Survival Acres: http://survivalacres.com/
- Mountain House Freeze Dried Food: http://www.mountainhouse.com/
- A gardening solution for small areas and urban living: http://www.vertigro.com/

Clearly, after you address your food reserve needs, you will want to turn your attention to power needs, communications, fuel, self-defense and other areas. Again, this is a life-long, ongoing process, but well worth every minute and dollar put into it.

Emergency cash savings are often recommended by financial professionals and the media, but they are rarely actually put into place by the investing public. In all the years that I have practiced, I can safely say that less than 5 percent (probably less than 1 percent) of the people that I have counseled had adequate cash reserves. Why is this?

It is certainly NOT that people do not know the value of saving. I regularly hear the desire, "I really need to save more!"

It could be that people lack excess funds to direct to saving...and this is becoming more of a reality as inflation eats us alive...but usually it is not for a lack of funds.

The reason that comes closest to the mark is that people lack discipline. However, that answer just raises other equally confounding questions like: So why do they lack discipline? Why aren't they motivated to save? And what will they do if they have an emergency and need cash?

After thinking on this for a while, counseling numerous clients and meditating on my own experiences, I believe the answer to this conundrum can be found in the way that the public views the concept of saving. And what is that view? In a word, futile.

We've all had the experience. We begin saving (for emergencies or any other good cause) and once a bit of capital is stored up, it gets spent, wasted or decimated by any number of less than noble reasons. Do that three or four times and you are likely to say: "What's the use?" as so many people have done. Add to that the easy access to credit and credit cards and you have the makings of a non-saving ethic.

Further, there is a problem in the way we view "emergency savings." Most people view them as some sort of static, well-funded nirvana that will never be disturbed. This is wrong. This wrong thinking is analogous to the "get out of debt" versus "managed debt" that was discussed in "Debt Management" section above.

Instead of trying to have an "Emergency Fund", you should strive rather to have emergency funding. Emergency funding is a process whereby money is stored, used and replenished on a regular basis. It is okay to have a targeted amount of money, say 6 months or 1 year of monthly cash flow, but don't allow that target to be so rigid that the failure to precisely meet (or keep) that targeted amount becomes a stumbling block to your constant attempts to build and use it.

Also try not to be Frugal Franny or Spendthrift Sam. Frugal Franny gets so convicted to saving that she NEVER lets any of it be spent...even on emergencies! And Sam is so ready to tap into his cash reserves that any reason satisfies his standard for an "emergency"..."Honey, it was a one-day only sale, I had to buy the chainsaw with the emergency money," says Sam. "But we live in a condo without trees or a yard," screams Honey!

Emergency savings are nothing more than the first line of defense that keeps an unexpected financial crisis from derailing your greater financial plan. If you experience a financial crisis and have to tap into your "emergency fund," your "debt management" process should simply add another "debt" to be repaid, the debt you have to rebuild your emergency savings.

How much cash you should have is a personal choice. It varies based upon how much risk you want to maintain in your financial plan. Clearly, just establishing a one-month's reserve is a minimum requirement. The strongest arguments can be made for having 6 months to one year of living expenses available in your "emergency fund." However, it is equally important to invest that cash in a vehicle that has an adequate yield to offset inflationary loss. Now it begins to become clear how debt management, emergency savings and the "be your own banker" strategy all work together to keep you in a financially secure position.

Insurance is for catastrophes. We have corrupted it by using it to cover any and all losses. Some even go so far as to try and profit from it. With that said, the first rule in coming up with the "proper insurance" plan is to re-commit to using insurance in the way it was intended, namely, for major, unanticipated, catastrophic losses and nothing else!

With the pervasive entitlement mentality and the "sissy-fication" of America, our re-adjustment to proper thinking is likely to prove hard. For example, my grandfather NEVER had health insurance until he was enrolled in Medicare. Today, we are told that health insurance is a right and should be universally provided. How did we go from a country of people independent enough to handle all of their medical bills to one where we aren't courageous enough to handle any of them...or at least to have a choice in the matter? Again, the first rule in coming up with the proper insurance plan it to re-commit to using insurance in the way it was intended.

But there is a more subtle, sublime and insipid change going on at our most fundamental level of thinking and belief. Call it the monetization of charity. Where once we relied on our extended family, church and community to help us in times of need, we now rely on government and corporate interests to do so. Predictably, they do so by throwing money at the problem (money they extracted from us) and without true charity. And who steps in to provide the love and compassionate touch that a hurting person

41

needs? That's right, the families, churches and friends, but now they do so without their financial resources.

Truly it is one of the strangest and cruelest of financial realities...and one of our own creation, even insistence. In our prideful quest to "not be dependent" on others, we have made everyone dependent on the least efficient, least compassionate of all institutions, the government and its corporatists lackeys. Breaking free of this circular conundrum will prove difficult indeed.

My own views of "proper insurance" are evolving. When I first started in the business, we were taught and it was presumed that everyone ought to have life insurance, health insurance and, if they could afford it, disability insurance. Then there was property and casualty insurance for our possessions. Liability insurance too. Malpractice insurance if your work required it. Then came Long-Term Care insurance...and the list grows longer. And if you want "insurance insurance", that is insurance coverage in case your primary insurance coverage is not enough, we have that too. It's called an "umbrella" policy. Wow!?!

After counseling a few people, I soon realized that most people simply could not afford all these insurances. Those who could (or tried to) called themselves "insurance poor". But the real travesty was how guilty my clients felt for not "doing the right thing" and "not having everything covered". Truly, the marketing and advertising gurus of the insurance firms had done a job on the American psyche!

However, the concept of insurance need not be this complex or costly. Insurance, in its most rudimentary form, is simply the pooling of money by a group to cover the unlikely potentiality of a catastrophe happening to one or two of the group.[9] The coverage can be minimal (just pay for the expenses of the catastrophe) or greater, depending on your goals. However, the more that you move away from the minimal i.e. a helping hand to get over hard times, the more the "insurance" will cost AND the more likely it will be that the system will morph into something undesirable like our current system.

So here are the steps to establishing your own insurance plan:

1. Decide what catastrophes you want to protect against;

2. Have an emergency fund sufficient to handle the exposures that you are retaining;

3. Look for insurances in the areas that you want covered[10];

4. Seek to cover the "catastrophe", not to get wealthy from an "insurance" claim;

5. Steadfastly refuse to have anxiety about the risks you have retained or about the natural exigencies of life.

---

[9] Even life insurance falls into this category. For even though everyone will die, not everyone will die pre-maturely. At least that is the theory, but theorists also recognize that life insurance has the flaw in it that if everyone were to die suddenly, there would not be sufficient funds to meet the claims. They call this "moral hazard" i.e. the hazard that they cannot live up to their promises.

[10] Remember this is just a "pool of money" and can be done on the family (or community) level or out-sourced to commercial interests.

In short, you can't cover it all and you shouldn't try to;

6. Have faith in God (see lesson #1 above).

As a general rule for personal financial planning, I still discuss life, health and disability insurance with my clients. However, by adjusting their perspectives to the proper role of insurance in their plan, my clients tend to take on more personal responsibility, eschew the high-priced "Cadillac" coverages and solve some of their insurance needs through other components of the financial plan. Here are some resources to get you started.

Proper Insurance Resources

1. *Die Broke*, Stephen Pollan. I give this book a qualified endorsement. I do not recommend it as a total financial planning guide based on some fundamental flaws in its basic reasoning, but the author is very good at sifting through the pros and cons of insurance and some available riders. He also gives good advice on how to structure policies properly.

2. For those interested in health insurance alternatives, you might consider looking into "medi-share" organizations. These are trying to revive the idea that communities can share in the needs of the individual. See, for example: http://samaritanministries.org/

3. Finally, for those interested in re-establishing the extended family as a solve for catastrophic losses,

there is a small but growing literature on those ideas. See, for example, *Restoring the Family* by Marian Horvat and other related books.

We move now to the third major component of an integrated financial plan, "financial stability".

But first, let's take a quick glance back and then ask a question:

- If you had a budget that kept you disciplined to spend less than you earned; and
- A savings program built into the budget that was always flowing money to your bottom line; and
- A strategy that further "forced" you to save money; and
- Then you added emergency provisions and emergency savings to handle any irregular, emergency situations that popped up in your life; and finally
- Had proper insurance to handle any catastrophes that were beyond the scope of your personal economy; then
- Wouldn't you think you had a pretty, darn good financial plan?

Well, in point of fact, I usually counsel my clients that IF they handle those first six items well, then the rest of financial planning usually takes care of itself. On the other hand, any client who complains to me that something is just not working in their financial house, I usually locate a problem in these first, fundamental areas. Truly, my Financial Report Card can be used as a priority list for those looking to start a plan OR as a thermometer for those looking to find out what's wrong with their plan!

So how do we make this plan even better? Well, we attempt to add more stability to the plan by addressing a couple of "what ifs". While previously we addressed the present (and projected the future) based on the current, known conditions of one's employment and earnings, now we move to addressing two uncertain, but potential future realities: bad/lost investments and loss of work.

Intrinsic worth items attempt to address the issue: What if my investments, including my cash savings, become worthless?

Now, intrinsic worth items are not some secret, specialty investment. Rather, "intrinsic worth item" is just a name I give to one type of investment where the value of the item resides inside the item itself and which can be held at home (or within reach).

Some would argue that all investments have value "in themselves", but in my experience I have found that few people evaluate whether the stocks they buy or the underlying companies invested therein really have a value commensurate with the amount of their investment. Further, most people have lots of "certificates" of value, that is, some paper proof that they own something of value somewhere, but how is this going to be of value to them if they cannot actually redeem those "certificates" for tangible items when necessary? This is what "intrinsic worth items" attempts to address.

Many people see this as an extension of the idea of buying emergency provisions. In other words, if it makes sense to have some extra food lying about the house, why not add a few other things that might come in handy during some catastrophic downturn? That is a perfectly fine way to view it, but the intrinsic worth category is more focused on investment items i.e. things that have value, that are appreciable, that are marketable and that can be used as a means of support.

Clearly, gold and silver fit the bill here and I advise my clients to build a stash of "hard currency" as a backup, reserve currency in the event that our paper currency implodes. However, one should not stop there. Tools and machinery fall into this category because they provide a means of earning a living. Farmland and livestock also are "intrinsic worth items" because they can be used to provide you and others with food. Firearms, munitions, jewelry, gemstones and collectibles all come under this category with the best being those that hold their value (or appreciate), are readily trade-able and/or which can be used as a means of support.

These days, it is not hard to find someone predicting the end of the economic world as we know it. Their facts and predictions are hard to refute. But whether that eventuality happens or not, the best way to sleep well at night is to be prepared for any weather by having an ample supply of intrinsic worth items. If you build an intrinsic worth reserve and the economic world does not collapse, then the worst thing that could happen to you would be to die with all these valuable things to pass on to your heirs! Not a bad deal for some current peace of mind.

Intrinsic Worth Resources

1. To purchase gold or silver bullion in bulk, I have found the most economical means is to buy directly from a mint, such as Northwest Territorial Mint (www.nwtmint.com).

2. If you prefer to invest on a smaller level, but in a more regular fashion, monthly, for example, then I find Silver Saver (www.silversaver.com) a very handy resource.

3. For things beyond "hard currency" you are only limited by your imagination.

Financial Stability: Alternate Earnings Method and Passive Income Generators

The second "what if" is simply this: What if you lose your current means of income? This could be through disability (which might make us take a second look at whether we are properly insured), but it is equally likely, if not more so, through the death of a spouse, divorce, being "downsized", laid off, fired, technologically replaced, made part-time or a host of other calamities. So, what if you lost your paycheck? What would you do?

I deal with this issue in two areas of the Financial Report Card: Alternate Earnings Method and Passive Income Generators (PIGs[11]). While these are similar, the thought process and the preparation necessary to achieve these ends differ. I will discuss each in turn.

An alternate earnings method is just what it sounds like, a way to earn money that is NOT your current employment. Let's say that you are a truck driver, but you also can play guitar. Voila, you have an alternate earnings method! Clearly, this truck driver could join a band, set up weekend gigs and make a nice supplemental income to his "regular" job.

Alternate earnings methods can be a hobby that currently pays you some extra money or simply a skill that you keep current

---

[11] I cannot precisely recall where I got this acronym or idea, but in trying my best to give attribution, I believe it was from the book, *The Perfect Business*, by Michael Leboeuf. My sincere apologies if another person deserves equal or more credit!

that can readily become a new employment. For example, my career has focused on financial planning and investment management. However, I am a licensed attorney. I perform my annual, continuing education and remain a member of the bar. Thus, while it would pain me greatly to return to active legal practice, I am perfectly qualified to do so.

I encourage all of my clients to develop whatever skills, hobbies and interests they have with an eye towards making them commercially marketable. It just makes sense to have a back-up earnings method.

Still, some (most?) of us are so busy just making ends meet that the idea of adding another thing to our list, even if it makes us more money, is simply unthinkable and unachievable. This is where passive income generators (PIGs) come in.

While alternate earnings methods focus on the individual's ability to produce more income through different means, a PIG attempts to increase our earnings without additional, personal effort…or, at least, without a LOT of effort.

The simplest example would be a limited partnership. In a limited partnership, you, as the limited partner, have the duty to pony up some cash to become a partner, but you have the right to income from the partnership and the requirement NOT to be actively involved in the management.

The purpose of this exercise is to encourage people to develop a means to generate income outside of their salaried job.

Whether or not it is "passive" in the strict sense is up to you. Rental properties are commonly used by my clients. Here, the amount of work required of them varies depending on whether they use a property manager or not. However, the income from the rental properties is not directly attributable to their efforts, but rather to their capital investment.

PIGs cause our inner entrepreneur to come out...or at least that is the purpose of it in my discussions with my clients. But whether a person immediately starts a profitable side business or simply thinks on it for a while, it is a worthy exercise none the less.

What are some other examples of PIGs?

- Royalty income-Want to write a book or invest in an oil well?
- Limited Partnerships-Got a brother or a friend looking for some capital to start up a business?
- Inventing and Innovation-Got the next great idea or product improvement?
- Banking?-If you have enough capital to begin loaning out, then the interest return can be quite nice...ask Bank of America.

Finally, two caveats. First, with PIGs, I am not trying to create in your mind some mythical scenario where money falls from the sky on your lazy bones. Even with PIGs, work is needed in due diligence, capital investment and continual vigilance.

Second, I am not advocating creating a second "employment" where you work by day in one trade and all night in another. No one could keep that pace and you should not try. Rather, you have to get trained in and accustomed to investing in businesses where you are involved, but not in charge or actively working.

Having an alternate earnings method and creating a PIG will go a long way in insulating us from the risks associated with salaried employment. They are also a great means to create financial stability in a wild and ever-changing economic world.

Alternate Earnings Method and Passive Income Generator Resources

1. For alternative earnings methods, a Google search will return many resources available for turning a hobby into a profitable business. Additionally, you may consider returning to school to hone different skills or learning any one of many trades.

2. For PIGs, I think the Rich Dad series of books, by Robert Kiyosaki, does a fine job in explaining the "entrepreneurial" mind and gives help in determining when you have started a "business" versus when you are just "self-employed" i.e. doing additional personal work. While I cannot endorse every idea of his, I think those books are a worthy read, in

particular, The Cash Flow Quadrant and the original Rich Dad, Poor Dad.

3. And, of course, there is *The Perfect Business* by Michael Leboeuf. See end-note #7.

The fourth and final component of the integrated financial plan that I call the "Financial Report Card" is Future Planning. Retirement funding, education funding and tax reduction strategies are the three topics that come under this category.

It may come as a surprise to many people that future planning and, in particular, retirement funding, comes so late in my analysis. After all, this topic seems to be the primary focus and pre-occupation of most other financial advisors. However, there is a simple, yet profound reason that I consider these issues lower on the priority list than the others. That reason is this: You may not live to see the "future".

The financial services industry has over-emphasized future planning and to the detriment of many people. Too many people are sacrificing immensely today for some supposed utopia of the future. I think this is a mistake for several reasons.

First, as stated earlier, no one is assured of a future, so some balance must be struck between living for today and planning for tomorrow.

Second, most future planning is generally built on faulty assumptions and creates unrealistic expectations. This over-emphasis on the future has forced people into two broad categories relative to their future expectations: Optimists and Pessimists. The Optimists believe that their future is going to be completely rosy with their financial sacrifices of today. The Pessimists believe that no amount of planning can thwart the "coming economic disaster" so why try. Neither is likely correct, but my goal in advising clients is simply not to exacerbate an existing over-emphasis on the future or what it means to the individual concerned.

Finally, current, future planning, especially as it pertains to retirement funding, is fraught with peril. Whether it be the all too common mistake of locking money in qualified, retirement accounts[12] or a person, at the behest of his advisor, putting the majority of his net worth in some of the riskiest places to invest, I believe the financial services industry has done a great disservice to their clientele...allegedly for some great, future moment that seems never to come.

Modern "retirement planning" is unnecessarily complex and could use a champion to de-mystify it. But rather than exhaust ourselves in deciphering the esoterica of qualified plans, annuities, trusts, pensions or what have you, let's instead follow the tried and true formula of generations past. They would tell us that, if we wanted to be financially prudent[13], we should save 10% of our pay every month.

---

[12] These are the 401(k)s, 403(b)s, IRAs, SIMPLEs, SEPs, etc. While these can have a place in a proper financial plan, for too many people, "investing" in these plans is "indistinguishable from dropping sixpence down a drain," as G. K. Chesterton once remarked.

[13] A colleague of mine told me that people need to strike the word "retirement" from their minds. His point was that "retirement" as we currently understand it is a rather modern notion and one that is likely to prove unsustainable. He said these were bad ideas, borrowed from failing governments and societies and that we emulate them at our peril. I agree and hence prefer the idea of "financial prudence" rather than the more speculative idea of "retirement." For more on the un-sustainability of these plans see my blog The Pension Pinch here: http://www.financialsanityin3lessons.blogspot.com/2010/10/pension-pinch-or-war-

Granted, this advice does not tell us where to put the savings or how to put them to work, but it proves itself pretty sound advice indeed. For example, a person earning an average wage and saving 10% of his earnings each month in an account earning 3% for 45 years (age 22-67) can retire at age 67 and have enough capital to continue at the exact same spending lifestyle for 11 years (age 78)[14].

True, this does not get him to current life expectancy, has not addressed potential major, medical bills, has not addressed inflation and leaves him penniless at age 78. But it is here that I defy any planner to present me with a plan that has 100% certainty of lasting to the client's death. In fact, the financial services industry is better known for disclaiming any "guarantees" and, as we all know from looking at any of their sales literature, "past performance is no guarantee of future results."

For some reason, we have placed entirely too much trust in institutions and faulty, future projections and too little trust where we have the best chance of success: ourselves and our families. Now we know that even our government is likely to default on their grand promises of Medicare and social security and I say that the best "social security" you are going to find is in the ones you love and those that love you. Consider setting up

---

of-ages.html

[14] I averaged some income figures from Wiki here: http://en.wikipedia.org/wiki/Average_Joe to come up with an average, individual income of $37,380. This person then saved $311.50 per month for 45 years at a 3% growth rate and amassed an account of $350,593.30. This account continued to grow at 3%, but was drained at a rate of $37,380 per year (the average income number). The account lasted just short of 11 years by 21 dollars.

your "retirement funding" plans with them as integral components and beneficiaries of your plan.

In sum, "retirement funding" involves the prudent saving of current dollars for future need. It should also include a multi-generational component where current earners (one's children) help those who can no longer work for the benefit of having residual assets pass onto them. Finally, our (the future retiree's) expectations should be shifted from being a desire to "stop working" to one wherein we continue to offer the support we can (babysitting grandkids to save day-care costs for the working generation) so that we receive our children's help and support in our old age. This, coupled with your savings plan, will give you the greatest chance at "retirement" success.

Finally, some people interpret my analysis of retirement planning as some negative commentary on the "market". Nothing could be further from the truth. I believe that market assets are a valuable tool and have a place in everyone's financial strategy. I simply maintain that we, as a society, are placing too much trust and emphasis in that arena to the detriment of more prudent planning options. Perhaps we simply need to change bumper stickers. Instead of the current and popular one that says, "I am spending my children's inheritance," maybe we would be better with one that read, "I am writing my kids INTO my retirement...and my will!"

Retirement Funding Resources

1. For the simple, yet powerful benefits of being a "saver", I suggest *The Millionaire Next Door* and, to a lesser extent, *The Wealthy Barber*.

2. Read "The Pension Pinch" on my blog; See endnote #9 below.

3. If you have IRAs and other market assets, I humbly submit my firm, The Fiscal Fitness Company, Inc. (www.tffco.com) as an investment manager. If you want inexpensive and fairly good asset allocation assistance with your 401(k), I suggest you check out www.smart401k.com. However, I do not recommend their affiliated company The Mutual Fund Store for the type of "retirement funding" suggested in this book.

When I first started out in the financial services arena, I regularly encountered clients who wanted to plan for college for their kids. Accordingly, I would set out running projections of how much college would cost in the future (at the time, education "inflation" rates were in the 7-8% range) and would report back some astronomical number that the family simply could not afford. Invariably, they went away sad and feeling like a failure. Eventually, I just quit running those projections.

Later in my career, when I discovered the "be your own banker system"[15] and that it could be used quite effectively to pay for college, I began working in that arena again…even opened a business dedicated specifically to it!

What I found was that just as modern "retirement" planning was loaded with erroneous presuppositions and faulty reasoning, so too was "education funding". The financial services industry had worked assiduously to convince every parent to "save for college". They even created education accounts that were analogues to retirement accounts: "education IRAs", "education savings accounts", "529 plans", "pre-paid college plans" etc. As usual, the goal of all this modern "financial planning" was to take the capital out of your hands and to hold it in their institutions.

The people who came to see me were either those who had never entered into this game because they recognized the

---

[15] See the section above entitled: "Money Management: Savings Program"

futility of it (not able to afford it) OR those who had simply put it off until the eleventh hour and needed a way to manage the costs now! We regularly produced a plan that did just that.

But the more interesting development that came out of this work was my discovery of the psychological and emotional distress that these parents had felt for years because they "were not saving for college." They were glad when I showed them a means to pay for college, but they were ecstatic when I told them that they did NOT have to pay for college and that there were better ways to ensure their child's academic success in a more efficient financial manner.

So let's try to escape the con job that the mainstream, financial press has put on us parents and assess why we most certainly do NOT have to pay for college and why, as a financial matter, it falls into the "future planning" category and lower on the priority list:

- We are talking about the future, and the child may not make it to the future (heaven forbid!).
- How do we know if the child is going to be an academic achiever?
- The child may not want to go to college.
- It is possible to pay your own way through school. In fact, many studies suggest that kids that do pay their own way do better![16]

---

[16] See, for example, http://www.forbes.com/sites/susanadams/2013/01/16/want-your-kids-to-succeed-dont-pay-for-their-education/

- The debate about whether a college graduate has better lifetime earnings than the vocationally trained rages on. In other words, it is hardly a settled issue.
- It is not an "either/or" proposition, that EITHER you, the parent, pay OR else the kid can't go to college. What about the "both/and" approach? We, the parent and student, will BOTH take some personal, financial responsibility for college costs AND we will both financially prosper from the result.
- Financial aid (grants, scholarships and loans) is an entire system devoted to "paying for college." Learning the ends and outs of that system is very important when structuring a plan for future tuition needs.

There are other reasons and each family, with their own set of values and conditions, will have their own. It is important, though, that we slay this beast, the ogre that says that we are financial failures if we don't "pay for college." Be liberated from this beast. Then, if you believe that college tuition is a worthy financial goal, approach it with the same sense that you approach retirement, that is, prudently save, create a family plan and encourage each person to do what they can towards the accomplishment of the goal.

Some general rules:

1. Avoid the education savings vehicles. They unnecessarily lock up your financial capital and usually work against you in the financial aid arena.
2. "Be your own banker" relating to student loans.
3. Don't get mired in future, overall cost projections. The facts are the facts, but are only facts when they are in the "now". If you begin paying for college and your plan was under-funded, so be it. If you can't afford the whole enchilada...eat half of it! The rest will have to work itself out and always will.

Education Funding Resources

1. http://www.finaid.org/ - Probably the best, overall, non-sales oriented website dedicated to informing parents and students about the financial aid system.
2. *Paying for College Without Going Broke*, Kalman Chany and The Princeton Review. An annually-produced, authoritative resource on the many issues that impact good, college-funding decision-making. However, I cannot recommend or endorse any of the service-providers that he suggests in the book. I simply have no experience with them.

The last of the "future planning" components is tax reduction or "taxes", but first let me make the standard, accounting disclaimer: I am not a CPA. Therefore, do not take what I say herein as tax advice for your specific circumstance.

More often than not throughout this book, I have taken an alternative position to what is recommended by the mainstream financial service gurus. I have done this not to be contentious or smart-alecky, but rather because I believe the industry has taken certain positions as "facts" which are not indeed facts. Then, based on those faulty assumptions, they propose faulty solutions. Regarding the issue of taxation, the situation is no different.

Like most Americans, I believe the tax code is unjust, over-reaching, likely un-Constitutional[17] and just plain stupid. Similarly, the idea of saving on taxes...getting one over on Uncle Sam...just makes my heart go aflutter! But making long-term investment and financial planning decisions based purely on a tax-reduction factor is nearly always a bad idea...notwithstanding what your CPA tells you. In fact, I would argue that most people, if not all, in the early years of their working lives are making a mistake if they are funding retirement vehicles to "save on taxes." Why? Because they are locking up much-needed capital and forcing themselves to become lifelong debtors.

---

[17] How can it be unconstitutional when the taxes are in the constitution? We'll have to leave that for another book, but I guess I will ask rhetorically: Do you think a king ever did anything un-monarchical?

64

Nelson Nash, the founder of the "be your own banker" system, expressed it to me this way:

If the government creates a problem...think of onerous taxation...and then offers you the solution to the problem...think tax-deductible retirement plans...aren't you just a little suspicious that you are being manipulated?

Aren't you indeed?

Instead, we create a whole cottage industry dedicated to finding ways in, out, around, over and through the tax system, but never suggest the most obvious remedy: change or abolish the internal revenue code and the IRS itself.

So entrenched is this mindset that when I attend estate planning conferences, the cynical joke that is regularly bandied about by the lecturers is when they call the latest tax act passed by congress the "CPA and estate-planning attorneys full employment act." Truly it is a shame that our "law" is so arcane as to need a special class of enlightened functionaries to interpret it for us.

Worse still, however, are the "solutions" this group brings us, the grand-daddy of which, is "TAX DEDUCTIBILITY". To be clear, I am not opposed, necessarily, to tax deductions, but rather to financial planning being based principally or significantly on tax deductions.

If all other factors support the idea of buying a home and then also getting the mortgage interest tax deduction, great. But don't buy a home to get that deduction! Similarly, if you have established solid money management/emergency preparation plans, added financial stability strategies,[18] and then have **excess capital** to invest in an IRA…plus you get the tax deduction…by all means start an IRA. But don't start an IRA just to get a tax deduction. In many cases, the money that you are locking up in an IRA will have many more valuable uses to you than the tax savings you will experience.

If you own your own business, the "tax deduction" dynamic does rise slightly in importance when making business spending decisions. However, it is still not an absolute decision factor. That is, don't make a business decision based solely on tax deductibility.

As I have gotten older and experienced the growth of the regulatory leviathan we call government, I have come to the conclusion that trying to deal with this monstrosity is a bit like "dealing with the devil." You may think that you are getting one over on the man for today, but you'll be dealing with the sad consequences of acquiescing to its illegitimate power forever thereafter. So perhaps it is time to change our goal from one of trying to reduce our taxes into one where we reduce the taxes themselves…and the bureaucrats that live on them!

Tax Reduction Resources

---

[18] See section 2, A-C.

66

1. If you have excess capital and have met all other financial planning suggestions, then finding means to reduce taxes through various, tax-deduction techniques is as simple as searching for such ideas via Google. Beware though, you are still "dealing with the devil" and may get burned. Proceed with caution.

2. Also, it is not hard to find avenues to begin working for a reduction in the size, scope and cost of government. However, I am opposed to most of the "tax reform" proposals being offered (FAIR Tax, National Sales Tax, VATs), at least in their current form, and would recommend against working for them. However, I believe the Liberty Amendment (www.libertyamendment.com) and the Audit the Fed (www.paul.senate.gov/?p=press_release&id=694) to be viable first steps in reigning in the federal government and returning us to a constitutional republic.

I will freely sacrifice to thee, and will give praise, O God, to thy name: because it is good. **Psalms 53:8**

LESSON THREE: SAVING (AND SPENDING)
WITH A PURPOSE

We come now to the final lesson in achieving financial sanity. In lesson one, we discussed the necessity of keeping the proper perspective on money, especially as it pertains to our eternal destiny. Lesson Three is an echo of that lesson and a means to apply those principles in the temporal world. In other words, Lesson Three is a practical application of Lesson One.

One of the ways that the ancient philosophers used to demonstrate that money was not the source of happiness was to show that people were only happy when they spent it, that is, gave it away for something else that they wanted. That rather simple and obvious fact made it clear that money was not the destination desired, but rather a point on the trip. So what is the destination? And more to the point, what is your destination?

The financial services industry has crafted an answer for you: Retirement. I know because just about everyone who walks into my office asks about it. The fact that "retirement" is a selfish and ultimately unsatisfying answer is just beginning to dawn on the baby boomers experiencing that reality. Not every retiree is disillusioned, but too many of them are experiencing one or more of a myriad of troubles in that so-called "paradise." The golden years have turned into golden tears!

A few of the tears:

- Many do not accumulate enough to retire (even if it were a laudable goal);[19]
- Most worry about running out of money;[20]
- There is "retirement adjustment" syndrome (which ironically recommends continuing to work...if only as a volunteer?);[21]
- Retirement loneliness;[22]
- Retirement boredom;[23]

If it were not so sad, it would be funny. Working all those years, saving up money to finally do what you always wanted to do and then discovering, "I don't know what I want to do, don't know if I have enough money to do it and don't have anyone to do it with!"

Worse still, every bit of experience, wisdom and skill that you did accumulate during your working years, instead of being highly praised and an asset to someone is...put out to pasture. Retirees often feel unloved and underappreciated and, indeed, we do not revere the aged. Shame on us.

[19] http://www.thedailybeast.com/newsweek/2013/05/06/american-retirement-in-free-fall.html
[20] http://www.usatoday.com/story/money/columnist/brooks/2013/07/15/retirement-savings-401k-pension-budget/2516191/
[21] http://health.howstuffworks.com/wellness/aging/retirement/10-tips-for-adjusting-to-retirement.htm
[22] http://retirementunplugged.com/retired-isolated-and-lonely/
23
http://online.wsj.com/article/SB10001424127887323415304578370270527673456.html

But Lesson Three is not about bashing the counterfeit purpose proposed for our lifetime savings, but to examine better alternatives. Again, what is your destination? If you do not want to end up unhappily "retired", then how do you want to spend your golden years? Or more fundamentally, can there be "golden years"?

In short, the answer is "yes"! All it takes is a goal, a little commitment and your devoted attention. It is best to make this a life-long commitment, but if you only start it in your senior years, it will still work. What is this wonder? In a word: Love. A special, outward, giving love we sometimes call charity...but that unfortunately connotes negative impressions in some due to those who have abused charity. Still, I hope you will hear me out on this.

In my practice, I have a section of my Financial Report Card devoted to "Making a Difference." Strange as it may sound, as I speak about budgets or saving or retirement or insurance or whatever other money topic arises, my clients are passive, at best, and bored at worst. It just isn't that interesting to them. I understand this. But the minute I mention "making a difference" with their money, they light up.

If I mention the "cost of freedom", the idea of using some of our money to preserve the freedom and prosperity we enjoyed growing up, I get into the most interesting political discussions you can imagine.

73

When I mention, "morally responsible investing", the idea that we should NOT put our hard-earned money to work with people, institutions or projects that are antithetical to our moral world view, my clients perk up with determined, but loving, righteousness and share their faith with me.

And when, in my meetings, I suggest "charitable giving", the idea of returning some value to the people and institutions that helped us along the way, nearly everyone I speak with says, "I always wanted to do that!" Then they tell me stories that would warm anyone's heart.

Charity is a motive force in human affairs. It is a purpose for which we can work and find joy in accomplishing. It is a worthy end. Thus it is, or ought to be, a goal in our financial plan. I do not believe there is a person alive who did not desire to "make a difference" when they started their working lives, but somehow that object was co-opted to the selfish end of living for oneself. However, it is living for others that will actually make us happy…wealthy or not!

The two great commandments that contain the whole law of God are:

- First, you shall love the Lord your God with your whole heart, and with your whole soul, and with your whole mind, and with your whole strength;
- Second, you shall love your neighbor or yourself. Matthew 22:37-39.

74

Lesson Three is all about planning for and accomplishing this! But we need not delude or deceive ourselves into thinking it must be some big splash or huge financial gift. That is the devil talking, trying to dissuade you from the undertaking. Remember the widow's mite (Mark 12:42). On the other hand, if you can endow a scholarship at your alma mater, feel free!

For our choice, we simply must focus on the "difference" we want to make and give regularly of our time, talents and treasure to that end. That difference could be directed to our home and our children. "Charity begins at home," my mother always said. So you might plan on developing land into a family community, building houses for everyone and sharing in the costs and upkeep of that community. What a mighty force that would be against the welfare state!

I use the "family farm" idea simply as an example. I cannot give you what YOU will be inspired about to love and cultivate. Only you can do that. But once you have that idea in your head and your heart, it will be the driving force behind your financial plan.

The only other caveat here is that we cannot let our plans become larger than God's plans. Remember Lesson One...and "Thy kingdom come, Thy **WILL BE DONE**..." But so long as we make sure that our charity corresponds with His, then we are on the right track to financial sanity.

With all my heart, I pray that God will bless you in that endeavor.

ADDENDUM

A couple of years ago I wrote an essay that I believe would be a worthy addition to this book. Here is that essay.

The Bankers' Bubble

Or

Why You Are More Likely To Wind Up Enslaved Than Retired

The modern world is full of dangers. But as is true with most perils, it is the ones unseen, or worse yet those considered neutral or even beneficial, that are the gravest. Quicksand can capture because it *appears* to the untrained to be normal earth. Hallucinogenic drugs consume the addict because the user enjoys the "trips" so much that he comes to *believe* they are good. Rarely does reason dissuade them of that opinion.

Yet in the case of quicksand or drugs, one still knows (or, at least, is told) to beware. How peculiar it is then that a danger that literally has world-wide, destructive implications could not only escape being labeled a danger, but could actually morph into something of "man's best friend" (sorry canines, you've been ousted). And to add insult to injury, we are not told to BE WARY, but to be involved. Truth is stranger than fiction.

In this brief essay I will set forth a number of facts that all lead to the conclusion that will be posited shortly, namely that we have called an evil, good, and will soon be suffering the consequences of that error. However, I will not set out the proofs of these facts, nor the technical aspects of the science underlying these truths nor the philosophic necessity of the conclusions drawn. Those activities I leave to the interested reader and the genuine seeker of wisdom. I welcome corrections and refutations where due.

So what evil have we called good? In a word: Interest. In older parlance it would have been called "usury", which still maintains its negative connotation. We still detest loan sharks. All other sharks we love and call bankers[24]! The fact that they both employ the same mechanism, albeit in different measure, should be our first signal to beware.

Now before the adherents of the Austrian, Keynesian, Chicagoan and other economic schools go into conniption fits, call me an idiot or, death of all deaths, old-fashioned or dismiss me as being completely unrealistic, I would like to offer two salient facts and then further clarify the various concepts[25] that converge to make interest the danger that it is.

First, as to the charge that I am an idiot (a charge that I may or may not contest), I would simply respond that your argument is not with me, but with Aristotle, St. Thomas Aquinas and dozens, if not hundreds, of other superlative minds who have

---

[24] This is not to imply that all "bankers" have evil motives or that any individual banker even intends the consequences set forth herein. Most have probably never even considered the implications of their work, a fact that itself is a sad indictment of our educational system and religious leaders.

[25] "Interest" is merely the bait on the hook. The dangers, the "hook" as it were, lie in a convergence of errors about the nature of money, debt and production, which will be set forth herein.

drawn the same conclusion that I now set forth. I did not dream up this accusation, but was bequeathed it. As I see it, the obligation is on you to refute their arguments with more than the casual dismissal that "they just didn't understand modern commerce." Really? And when did commerce so change as to refute the immutable laws of human nature?

Second, the belief that a world without interest is unrealistic or economically non-viable ignores the patent reality that there was a ban on usury (classically understood as any lending at interest) for nearly all of the Christian era, the official ban only being lifted by the Church in 1918. Can we realistically conclude that there was no economic progress[26] for all of those centuries?

No, we live in an easy-money, debt-based economy that is divorced from the real world of economics. Worse still, it was designed that way by the moneyed interest. Worst of all, it can only lead to the enslavement, and ultimately to the destruction, of the common, working man.

Let me assure you that this is not a fantasy. It is not hyperbole. What was built and is now being perpetuated was the biggest fraud in the history of mankind. Being a fraud, it is immoral. Being immoral, it is offensive to God. Being offensive to God, yet all the while being accepted and praised by man, is

---

[26] This notion of "progress" seems to be where many of the arguments go awry. "Progress to what end" is the pertinent inquiry whereas material multiplication (and alleged betterment) seems to have become the end. This issue will be further addressed in the area where "interest" is further clarified.

why it will end in destruction. So, like the prophets of old, though I am hardly one, I must say repent and turn back to God.[27]

And as with any repentance, we must first acknowledge and confess our sins....

---

[27] As a Catholic, I will prove my charge of the immorality of the current system from Christian sources. However, because the conclusions I draw will be apparent and clearly corresponding to reality, I do not believe that any person of good will would doubt the validity of the conclusions merely on the basis of rejecting my faith.

There was a time when the term "easy-money" was only in the parlance of gamblers and crooks. With the advent of "every man a usurer mentality", it is the quest of every red-blooded American. Something has changed, but what? And is there anything wrong with it?

What has changed is easy to state, but not so easy to understand...or, at least, to understand its importance. I have had dozens of conversations about this change and its consequences and the discussion always devolves into esoterica. Ultimately, the person says, "so what," thinking that our discussion might have import to a college, economics professor, but certainly not for them. Hopefully my past communication failures have sharpened my expository skills and I will be able to demonstrate why this issue has such great importance to every individual on earth.

So what has changed? Briefly stated: The essence and nature of money and, therefore, our right relation to it. Or even more simply, our understanding of:

- What money is; and
- What its proper use is.

So what is money? Essentially it is a storehouse of our production. And its corresponding and proper use is supposed to be a means by which the value of the things we have produced is held in a form that is more easily tradable (a medium of exchange, in economic language). For example, a rice farmer could lug into town hundreds of pounds of rice to do his weekly shopping (the old barter system) or he could sell his rice for money (presumably for the value he thought fair) and use the money to trade instead. The money is supposed to store the value of his rice until he exchanges it for something (or several things) he believes are of equal value.

As with all storehouses, you want to watch out for rats and thieves[28] who steal things from the storehouse when you are not watching. But that's another issue. For now the foundational point to remember is that money is a storehouse of your production. Money is a representative of your production.

Now, in the story of our exile from paradise, we read, "with labour and toil shalt thou eat thereof all the days of thy life…In the sweat of thy face shalt thou eat bread till thou return to the earth, out of which thou wast taken…." Genesis 3:17-19. In punishment for our disobedience, the Divine declared that our work, our production, would be toilsome. It is not an option; it is a fact of our fallen state. Anyone who has truly worked would confirm the statement.

Perhaps now we can begin to see why the "easy-money" mentality is such a temptation. At its core, it is an attempt to

---

[28] The rats are politicians who impose unjust taxes and the thieves are bankers who steal through fraudulent monetary policy, namely inflation and fractional reserve banking.

escape the divine reprimand. And to escape the Divine is to seek refuge where?

But underlying the inherent lie of "easy money" is the fallacy that money is wealth. As stated earlier, money is a sign or representative of one's production (earnings or wealth), NOT the production, earnings or wealth itself. To seek "money" as wealth (or to equate money with wealth) is to misconstrue the very nature of money. Further, to acquire money without the corresponding production[29] is nothing less than theft. Hence, my claim that it is immoral.

Admittedly, this is a subtle point: the divorce of a sign from what it <u>signifies</u>. So to make clearer the dangers of such a break-up, let's consider the following example.

In olden days whenever a king wanted to issue a proclamation or law, he would stamp the document with his ring. This stamp in wax authenticated that the proclamation was indeed the will of the ruler. In short, this was the "sign" of its authenticity and people gave it due deference because the sign guaranteed that it was indeed what it signified, the will of the sovereign. But what if a close, royal advisor was able to steal or periodically use the royal seal at his own whim? In other words, what if an advisor could forge royal documents? It is clear to most people that under these circumstances, a forgerer such as this would be able to fool

---

[29] The issue of whether or not capital (money) can be put to "productive" use and therefore warrant an interest payment will be addressed later. The salient point I labor to make here is that we have ceased WORKING for wealth and expect rather our wealth (erroneously equated with money since it is divorced from production) to WORK for us.

the population into abiding by false edicts by taking advantage of what the seal signifies (the will of the sovereign) by the misuse of the sign (the stamp of the sovereign). This very real danger exists whenever one breaks the connection between signs and their signification.

Accordingly, in saner times, money was understood to be a SIGN of a man's production and, to make sure that this link was not broken,[30] the money itself was backed by a commodity whose "production value" was easily ascertainable and not easily manipulated. "As good as gold" rings true because the common man understands that it (the gold) was not created by some artifice, but rather by real production. It takes effort to get gold from the ground and we innately know that effort is compensable. "The laborer is worthy of his reward."[31]

But now we have severed the link between labor and reward. We seek the reward (money, the sign) without the labor (the production, what money signifies). Worse still, we equate the "sign" (the money) with what it "signifies" (our production). We are trading in forged documents! And by falsely equating the sign with what it is supposed to signify, we all seek and horde the

---

[30] I emphasize this point to answer the common man's objection: "But I do work for my money." I admit that work is being done, but two distinctions must be made: 1. That the work being done is truly "productive" and 2. That the money received for said work is ALSO representative of productive activity. In other words that it is TRUE money. To make the point even clearer, why is counterfeiting a crime? Because it puts into circulation FALSE money. So do we now have FALSE money circulating under our current fiscal and monetary policies? That is one question at issue.
[31] 1 Timothy 5:18.

counterfeit signs of wealth and eschew the real (the actual) production of wealth.

This destruction of the distinction between sign and signification has so confused the issue of money and wealth as to make rational discourse nearly impossible, hence my need to continuously clarify the above paragraph with parentheticals. Truly this is a "diabolic disorientation". Therefore, I will use the word "marker" in lieu of the word "money" as we go forward to maintain the distinction between the signs of wealth and the wealth itself (which, to emphasize again, is the actual production and the things produced).

Now this severing of the link between the real thing, our production and value of our labors AND the symbol of those things, our money or the markers of wealth, is principally due to the concept of interest.

Imagine a friend telling you that he was taking a trip to Chicago. Then, a few weeks later when you encounter him and ask him how he liked Chicago, he says, "I didn't get there, I only got halfway." Curious, you then ask: "And what is halfway to Chicago?" To which he replies, "Nothing, but it was great!"

Now imagine having that same conversation over and over again with nearly every person you meet. I believe that you would start to think that everyone was insane OR that you needed to get halfway to somewhere!

This perverse absurdity is the essence of modern pseudo-Capitalism, the complete confusion of means and ends. As stated before, money is a <u>medium of exchange</u> (because it is a marker signifying production). In other words, it is an <u>intermediate step</u> in a <u>completed transaction</u>. It is a point on a trip, but not the destination. It is "halfway to Chicago". And need it be said that there is no value in getting halfway to your goal UNLESS it is just another step on your way to the goal?

---

³² A mentor of mine once said that "isms" are defined more by what they deny rather than what they assert. So "materialism" is not the affirmation that there is matter, which is all too obvious, but rather that there is nothing but matter. It is the denial of the spiritual. Similarly "capitalism" is not a system that affirms capital, the money, stock and equipment used in the start-up and continuation of a business, but rather a system that maintains that there is nothing but capital which will be employed by businesses for profit. In other words, the "capitalism" that I criticize will be that distortion of business that makes the accumulation and maximization of capital its only interest. Regarding the other side of this false dichotomy, socialism, I subscribe to the words of our Holy Father: "No one can be at the same time a sincere Catholic and a true socialist." Pope Pius XI, Quadragesimo Anno.

But the curiosity is not that someone would stop halfway on a trip. There are many plausible, even valuable, reasons for doing so. Rather, the more curious notion is that the halfway point has become the new end[33] and the claim that this "end" is "great" despite "nothing" being there.

The fact that the goal of most people is to accumulate a large pile of markers shows just how insidious and pervasive this distortion has become.[34]

So what makes a man not only stop "halfway to Chicago," but claim that the nothingness that is there is "great"?

Well the truth is there was an attraction "halfway to Chicago" that was so interesting that they gave it that very name: interest. Never mind that it distorted the purpose of money, turning it into an end in itself, as discussed above. To fix that small problem, all that was necessary was to invent a false economic philosophy (capitalism[35]), dress it up with nonsensical "scientific" terms (time value of money, for one[36]) and then let

---

[33] This point cannot be stressed enough. It is equivalent to claiming that reading half a book, watching half a movie or playing half a game is the proper end of those activities. And while we often do stop these activities half way, only a fool or a liar would say that we had FINISHED.

[34] I am not here arguing against the accumulation of wealth, but of markers (and more particularly money for money's sake, especially when it is false money). If you still equate the two, go back to the previous section. On the contrary, so long as the money accumulated is truly representative of past production (i.e. wealth), then the accumulation of money will be a necessary step until the party is ready to exchange for other produced items. What is being argued against is the delight and desire to make this accumulation the terminus of the trip. How this chicanery was accomplished is the conclusion I hope to draw, but which I have not yet proven.

[35] See footnote 9.

[36] I will be assailed from all sides for this assertion, but its defense will have to be left for another essay.

nature take its course, that nature being that man would prefer earning without work rather than exerting himself.

Ideas have consequences, so they say, and if this escape from work was the only consequence of the concept of interest, it would be bad enough. But the deadliness of usury only begins there. Our current economic woes are inextricably tied to that original error and the coming cataclysm was prophesied long ago when St. Paul warned us: "The desire of money is the root of all evils."[37]

And if interest's allure is based upon the "root of all evils," then pseudo-capitalism is the full flowering of that most pernicious error, destined to end in self-destruction because it encourages surplus for surplus' sake, accumulation for accumulation's sake, consumptionism, debt and the passing of responsibility for production to some unknown class of people.

---

[37] 1 Timothy 6:10

"Money, like wine and wheat, is consumed by being used. Hence the use of the thing cannot be separated from the thing itself. Consequently he who, besides requiring back the thing [the money or item lent], also extracts a price for its use, sells and gets paid for what <u>does not exist, which is unjust</u>."[38] [Emphasis added]

After first reading these words of St. Thomas Aquinas years ago, I confess to having grave doubts about their validity. Frankly, it went against everything I "knew" about economics and "capitalism". While I objected that "money could be used as capital and put to productive use thereby justifying the interest payment," I discovered that St. Thomas already denied the validity of that objection.

Worst of all, I hardly comprehended St. Thomas' argumentation. A condition that apparently extends to every capitalist apologist who regularly dismisses his objections as being out of touch, not in accord with modern economic thought or as simply a product of a medieval mind. But eventually, through hard work, study and prayer, I came to understand and agree with his conclusions. I will try to elucidate them here.

But before we embark upon a more thorough examination of the truths he stated, let's cut right to the chase and ask ourselves the tough question (don't worry, it's a simple answer): Can there

---

[38] St. Thomas Aquinas, IIa, IIae, Q. 78, a. 1, as quoted in The Framework of a Christian State, E. Cahill, S. J. p. 50.

exist such a thing as a "Never-Ending Expansion"? Or, if you prefer a more concrete and specific example of the same question: Can the stock market[39] forever increase by 10 to 12 percent?

If you correctly answered "no", then you have begun to see the wrongness and evil that is implicit in the first usurious transaction. Moreover, whether or not you see the connection, the people who do believe there can be a "never-ending expansion" have brought our country to the brink of destruction with TRILLION dollar debts and deficits! But I digress.

St. Thomas did not need to wait for the evidence to bear out the truth that was evident in his mind, that "interest" was an abuse of the essential character of money and that anyone who required it "sells and gets paid for what does not exist, which is unjust." One injustice was enough to dissuade him from endorsing that course. If only we had such principled character in our time.

Of course the classically trained minds, ever seeking the truth through distinction, did finally conclude that there could be a case when "interest" might be justifiable[40], but the moment that door was opened, lesser minds threw off the discipline of philosophic inquiry and went full-throttle towards the aberration that is enslaving us now.

To demonstrate how this happened, we must imagine an admittedly simple economy immediately prior to the introduction of interest and the results thereof.

---

[39] Only one of many of the manifestations of this erroneous, economic thought.
[40] The payment from future profits derived from the use of non-consumable, capital items.

So let's imagine a handful of farmers living in proximity, each subsisting on their own production. One farmer, Al, just happens to have a spare horse (capital item) that is not essential to his production. At the request of a second farmer, Bob, Al loans this horse to Bob so that Bob can get his own field plowed. Bob promises to pay Al part of his corn production (interest) for the use of the horse. Whether Al wanted, needed or desired the surplus corn payment is irrelevant.

At harvest time, Al has his own produce plus the corn that Bob paid him. Al finds that he has an excess of corn, so he heads to town to sell the corn and an idea hits him: "Why don't I buy a third horse and rent that one out too? Maybe I won't have to plant corn at all on my own farm (thereby saving work) and can help another farmer with a plow-horse." This he does. At the next season, Al leases his horses to Bob and Charlie at a slightly higher interest than last year since he has more horses to feed.

Bob and Charlie respond by over-planting corn and reducing some other crops (market distortion) because they know that they will have to pay Al out of their surplus. This they do and this season passes much like the last and Al is paid his interest payments as planned.

Before long, Al decides that the best course of action for him is simply to continue buying horses and leasing them to needy farmers. He does not see any market distortion; he is not interested in what is being produced in abundance and what is being more scarcely produced. All he knows is that if he can continue this operation, he will be able to "earn" a living off of keeping a stable of horses and that his back-breaking plow days are over.

But somewhere down the line, Bob recognizes Al's game and decides to start playing it himself. Bob says: "Before, we were all farmers. Now Al calls himself a rancher, which I guess is a fancy word for someone who doesn't work, but gets paid for his horses. I think I want to be a rancher too." (Human nature and the beginning of the divorce of the sign from the signification of money).

Here the complexities of the economy start mounting and we will have to end the story. But, suffice it to say, it does not matter whether Bob goes into direct competition with Al (i.e. undercutting him on lease costs) or if he begins the ranching business in another town (thereby initiating the disrupting influence there) to see that eventually the demand for horses will grow, the glut of corn will continue, the scarcity of other produce will escalate, the multiplication of the "system" will result and that the "never-ending expansion" has begun[41].

Only it is NOT never-ending.

Though it is difficult to do so, imagine EVERYONE owning horses for lease to non-existent farmers[42]. However, the

---

[41] I am NOT here arguing that all people should be subsistence farmers. And I do recognize that this process has resulted in division of labor and other systemic benefits. But what I am stating rather emphatically is that the unregulated nature of it is leading to catastrophe.

[42] The finite nature of the need for horses has caught up with the ranchers and

reason it is difficult to imagine is because we no longer deal in horses or produce or any other real asset, but with markers. We lease money. Worse still, the "interest" we charge on the leased money creates more money...for LEASE. If you cannot hear the KABOOM, keep listening. It's coming.

It shows in our "production" too. Nearly everything we make is disposable. Why? Because the financiers must have you trading markers incessantly. They must force someone to buy corn when there is a glut of corn. We are sold items with "planned obsolescence" so that we will continually purchase new computers, cars, washing machines, telephones, refrigerators, you name it. Of course, our new purchases would occur naturally when things broke down, but in the never-ending expansion, that time frame has to be compressed to the shortest duration possible because an interest payment has to be made.

Then there is the pressure on businesses. Because the "loan" is the constant companion of the entrepreneur, he must cut costs and maximize profits to improve the bottom line and keep happy the creditor. When this proves impossible to do and still provide adequate wages to the employees, he will simply move the "production" to slave labor countries like communist China.

Compulsory healthcare is just the latest evidence that slavery is coming. You MUST buy, whether you want it or not, because those running the bankers' bubble know that any opt out

---

destroyed their business and possibly their lives due to the false notion of the never-ending expansion.

of their "economy" by the common sense, working man brings the whole phony system crashing to the ground.

The reason that the Bankers' Bubble will necessarily end in slavery for most of mankind is simply this: That we have convinced the better part of five generations that they can be a non-working "rancher," whose "horses" are nothing more than electronic digits that allegedly produce all of the purchasing power they will ever need. These same generations care not who produces the products that they will consume because they have a "right" to pensions, retirement, interest etc., so someone better get to work. Sadly, the notion of real work and true money in their brains has long since atrophied.

We are doing worse than selling that which "does not exist." We are **promising** that which may not, and very likely cannot, exist...all on the backs of some future generation or "foreign" people. So if selling that which "does not exist" is, as St. Thomas says, unjust, then promising that which may not exist at the expense of another is certainly diabolic.

This is the Bankers' Bubble. And the immediate and most efficacious response to it is simply this: Quit dreaming about retirement and set your family on the noble and true path of genuine production and economics.

BIBLIOGRAPHY

The Financial Planning Workbook, A Family Budgeting Guide (Christian Financial Concepts 1990), Larry Burkett

The Catholic Answers Guide to Family Finances, Phil Lenahan

Crown Financial Ministries, www.crown.org

Becoming Your Own Banker, R. Nelson Nash

Infinite Banking Institute – www.infinitebanking.org

http://www.financialsanityin3lessons.blogspot.com/

The Creature from Jekyll Island, G. Edward Griffin

Restoring the Family, Marian Horvat

Die Broke, Stephen Pollan

The Perfect Business, Michael LeBoeuf

Rich Dad Series, Robert Kiyosaki

The Millionaire Next Door, Thomas J. Stanley and William D. Danko

The Wealthy Barber: Everyone's Common-Sense Guide to Becoming Financially Independent, David Barr Chilton

Paying for College Without Going Broke, Kalman Chany and The Princeton Review

INDEX

401(k), 55, 58, 71

403(b), 55

Alternate Earnings Method, 22, 49-50, 52

"Be your own banker", 30-31, 33, 40, 59, 62, 64

Budget, 25-28, 45, 71-72

Burkett, Larry, 25-26

Chany, Kalman, 62

Charitable Giving, 73

College, 59-62, 79

Cost of freedom, 72

Debt Management, 22, 32-34, 39-40

Education Funding, 22, 54, 59, 62

Emergency Fund, 32, 39-40, 43

Emergency Preparation, 22, 24, 35, 38, 41, 65

Emergency Savings, 39-40, 45

Envelope system, 26

Financial Stability, 22, 45, 49, 52, 65

Future Planning, 22, 24, 54-55, 59-60, 63

Genesis, 13, 80

Georgias, 14

Griffin, G. Edward, 32, 34

Hard Currency, 47-48

99

http://www.financialsanityin3lessons.blogspot.com/

www.tffco.com

38626281R00060

Made in the USA
Lexington, KY
17 January 2015